Under Our Knees Are Yellow Leaves

Lilia Skopintceva

BookLeaf Publishing

Presentation by *BookLeaf Publishing*

Web: www.bookleafpub.com

E-mail: info@bookleafpub.com

ISBN: 9789357610353

First edition 2022

ACKNOWLEDGEMENT

I'm very grateful to writer Kevin Cosgrove for his help editing these poems.

Fam

Your soft skin, your inner smile.
Touching, but be worried:
It’s better we went somewhere for a while.

Let us hide near this street
Remove our feet
You are tender
And this
I will always remember

You are my mirror:
Same body, same thoughts, same sorrow.
Our courage, our reflections
That they would secretly borrow.

Let them say: "It is not good".
Let us be perfectly misunderstood.

God would forgive our desires,
Let’s pretend we are ready for hell,
Knowing these rules are not fair.
But for how long will we care?

The Kingdom of Crooked Mirrors

What do you see? Tell me.
All of it is strange...
Over an abyss, under a lie,
We are playing for a while.

Fake smiles, the same faces.
How much longer can it all last?
Ideas of a mediocre parade
With flattering speeches as masquerade.

The authorities are bestial.
Their glances are full of firm steel.

Uneven waves of hugs,
Bursts of handshakes
And, in the back, volleys of curses.
Kingdom of masks,
Baltasar Carnival.
Yes, you are still there —
In the kingdom of crooked mirrors.

Who is an enemy to you,
Who is your friend?
Some don't know it here,
Some can’t be sure there.

Caviar, and wine and maybe ...
Will we play at dominos?
Will we bet at the casino?
Here you can see women's eyes full of a fire.
In them you can easily drown and never tire.

What else have you not seen here?
Wealth, jokes and overall fun,
But one might see a hand holding a gun.
Feeling desperation and sorrow,
If you go deeper,
You will deal with a pure horror.

Everything here you can arrange,
Even buy an eternal light,
But not a heart that does not change.

Fireflies

I smashed into your life and you were shocked.
I wanted love and you did not.
Oh, the story is so old,
When someone comes into your world.

I observed your inner light
That was shining so bright,
But I did not mind ending up blind.
And you said: “My skin is too tight,
I don’t feel alright”.
Then you went into the woods in your usual
way:
Straight and then right.

Maybe I was wrong,
And there was no need to moan.
Our lives are not only snow-white,
And no matter who was right,
The fireflies shine for us
Every night.

Something Inevitable

"What's the point of forgetting, if it's followed by dying?"
(Joseph Brodsky, 'A Song')

And in his words
There is so much that is true —
These are vulnerable, soulful chords.

One can forget
And just stay laughing out loud.
Then one can regret,
When it's time to not be proud.

When a dream has gone,
With nothing left behind,
It is harder than the heaviest stone -
With only new meanings to find.

In the darkest moment of fate
One cannot underestimate.
The shy and tiny ray of a hidden light
Will appear and immediately be gone.
Therefore leave the rest of your hopes behind.

Under Our Knees Are Yellow Leaves

The wind is blowing,
The autumn is coming.
The body is shaking
The mind was mentally breaking

See all this grass here,
It is already not green
And leaves on the ground
Are left to be seen.

Always painful to be growing,
Always painful the not-knowing.
Not all things could be resolved,
Not all people could be loving.

The wooden houses were left behind us,
Night whispers, rain dropping silently,
And this damn pain in our necks.
Under our knees are yellow leaves.

Time brings the shadows of tears,
Then disappears between dark trees.
Everything is slightly fading away,
Confusingly hid in the morning dawn

And only yellow leaves are under our knees.

No Name

A light, then darkness.
Feeling empty inside.
A fireplace and wine,
And it seems alright.

Where are we all going to in the end?
One can hear and feel only what one can never
understand.

Full of darkness on a typical night,
Weakness and power are under one eternal light.
We can see a candle flame,
But this is all far from a game.

The forgotten shadow wanders in the haze.
A desperate cry is heard like from those lost in a
maze.
The mirror is broken
And no one will get away unless woken.

We stopped time,
Which won't prevent the crime.
Someone had left and taken away the light.
Boiling tea is cooling down in the teapot
And the moon is so visible in this night.
It will be better like this
Or maybe not.

On The Beach

Not susceptible to anything and anybody,
I go where the limitless sky and the sea
Merge together in their azure colours,
Where the gulls scream and fly very close to
you.

I go where the noise of waves sounds
Like the most relaxing music ever,
Where all thoughts leave your mind forever,
Evaporating into nowhere,
Creating an infinitely pleasant emptiness in my
head.

Having spread my hands
Like I'm trying to reach the distant sky above,
I fall on the rough surface of the sand,
Looking into the distance, at the horizon,
Feeling an irresistible sense of endless freedom.

A light cool wind gently blows,
Giving rise to a scattering of goosebumps on my
body.
The air is saturated with freshness.
It gives strength when one inhales it.
Closing my eyes, looking into a blue sky

With its slow and creamy clouds.
Standing calm for a second and then
Catching a serene feeling of happiness
Which fully engulfs my whole inner body
Like a tight and warm cocoon

Under Your Skin

The first step is the hardest one:
Tears, excitement, emotions,
But you aren’t going to run,
Feeling dizzy to touch
And hot as hell,
It’s still good with the proper approach.

Shaking in your hands,
Heart beating, goosebumps, pulsation —
All this vice’s closest friends.

Breathe quieter
So that no one can hear.
Going deeper into body and mind
To warm a cold soul.
Do you feel a share of the risk?
Don't move smoothly
Otherwise we will be bored.
Being under your skin is like soaring to the sky
And gives a final happiness.
The body is in a hurry
Towards sweetest surrender.
Whispering in the ears
Will wash away our fears.

Extremes Meet

They were very different:
Like a snow cold winter is different
From the green and warm summer;
Like yin and yang or white and black;
Different as when one is about to build
And another is about to wreck.

She loved spring and Paris
And to be open to him —
He loved autumn and Moscow;
His emotions were dim.

She adored dogs, bunnies and cats —
He could not even stand pets,

She liked mysterious movies by David Lynch —
He loved cartoons about The Grinch.

She was constantly laughing, was fun overall —
He had a mood that was grim above all.

She used to drink coffee — black as a demon,
He always chose green tea with a lemon.

She used to drive at a high speed around the city,
He preferred to be at home, watching TV
without pity.
She loved long teasings and to be in illusions —
He preferred quickies and to scoff at people's
delusions.
She loved to read Murakami, Márquez and
Dante.
He barely knew who they were and not even
wonder.

Every night they went out onto the balcony
To look at the sky above.
An immeasurable number of stars flickered over
their incompatible heads,
And left them with a feeling of eternal
happiness.

Dreams

In my dreams, a hair blowing on the cold air.
I confused the smell of men's parfum
With the memorable aroma of southern seas.

The night's full moon is like a not-yet-ready
pancake.
You would fall asleep so quickly
And the conscious need for a fully-fledged
dream
Would force you to immerse yourself in the
world of fantasies
And utopian visions.

When one is about to determine just when one
falls asleep
All efforts may be in vain.
Sleep is generally incomprehensible yet
amazing,
Ridiculous and beautiful,
Strange and terrible at the same time.
You will wake up in the morning
And for a time you will not recover quickly
After all those pictures you were shown last
night.
And sometimes you are incredibly sorry

That these paintings were just your dream.
But when you try to remember those fragments,
And write them down as soon as you can,
You might understand the subconscious things
Which were carefully hidden from strangers'
eyes
And from yourself.

The Music Of The Rain

Turn on the light
As in the dark I remember more than you.
No more words
As just a look
Will bring me to mind.

There are a heaven and a hell in your eyes
And everything is like before
And those words cannot be forgotten.

Bring everything up again.
Remember and understand
Listening to the whispering of the wood
And the music of the rain playing loudly outside.

And this only is what can be understood:

Read me like an open sheet.
Light me like a candle,
In silence and in darkness,
Under the proper cover of the night.

Forbidden Fruit

Love it and hate it.
Put it away and then be attracted again.
Completely dissolving,
Remembering that "this is not mine"
Then cooling down
Just for a moment.

Only to start gaining speed
On the sweetest autobahn
With a strong desire for forbidden fruit
And an indestructible craving to taste it deeply.
To forget about what will happen tomorrow,
In a year, in ten years.
Only this instance —
The feeling of tasting this fruit
Is in your whole body and soul,
And this feeling evokes only
That which does not belong to you.
It captures and absorbs the whole,
Leaving behind a muddy trail of desires
And reflections.

The doors have closed, you think forever,
But you are wrong.
Later the sunset will come.
This is the time when the sun and the sky are magic beautiful.
Finding yourself again in a vicious circle,
Just because you want it.
And it will end only when the sun stops setting,
And then there will be only eternal dawn.

Flying In The Clouds

See the wings behind your back.
Open them, open your eyes wide
And the heavens will become closer
For you and me.
Let's fly there,
So that not a single tear falls again
From a child's face.

Flying into the clouds,
Under the breath of the wind in our dreams,
The flight will last forever
Until your eyelashes flinch.

We will arrive at the sun.
We will rush towards the hot rays.

Let's make a wish and let it be fulfilled.
Heaven will lift our sadness
And we will hear the music in silence.

Give me your smile.
Feel happiness inside.
Warm me with your warmth
From a hidden fire of the soul.

Where the wind whips the hair,
Where angels hear our voices,
Where we are as if in a wonderful dream,
There I will tell my dream to you.

The sun plays with gentle rays.
We seem to stand at the gates of paradise.
Unearthly songs birds sing to us.
Stars fall onto our lashes.

Sweetest Delusions

We think we are beautiful —
But no one admires us.

We think we are clever —
And make so many mistakes.

We think we are brilliant —
But haven't done anything very worthwhile.

Maybe we are thinking too much?
No matter what, however,
We move forward forever.

We will be ready to make the sea shed tears,
To be pricked by thorns without fears,
To drink the poison from the glass,
To join the street strikes of another class.
All this just to make the world believe in us.
We will love like the first time.
We will live as if it's our last day.
Maybe something will go wrong,
But maybe it will be okay.

Telephone Calls

These 'old school' phone calls —
We are so close and so far away.
At a late hour,
When the daylight went out long ago,
Sometimes words are needed
And sometimes they are not so important.

Old letters are too dangerous to read,
Old calls are nostalgically memorable
Like that old sugar reed
Which was planted near your house
And to remember all this is unbearable.

A fresh wind is playing with my hair,
Calling you but I know you do not hear.
The river of hope in the soul flows smoothly
Like tears on cheeks.
I feel your never-spoken sadness.

The world has become different beside you.
A fire went out in the eyes
And left pain in the heart instead.
An eternal abyss is between us again
And only your voice is still in my head —
As on a broken telephone line.

Solitary Man

Once upon a time,
There was a man living by the coast side
Under its constant smell of fresh limes.

He was alone, but his loneliness
He could easily bear.
He was free as a bird,
Wild as a manul cat,
Lonely as an ostrich,
Hiding his head in the sand.

He had deep blue eyes.
People around him said they were cold as ice.

He barely left his house.
His only friend was a mouse
They said.

Once he sat under the deep blue sky
Glancing as if he were asking "why?"

But silence was an answer to him
So he sighed and went to swim.

Suddenly the lightning struck
And the thunder broke the cold silence of the night
And the heavens swallowed him outright.
After that the heaviest rain gladly poured onto the ground,
As if it were nature's sign of relief and inspiration.
And the world became one step closer
To salvation.

Seaside Town

In a seaside town
Seagulls are screaming.
Waves are raging.
Every summer someone goes swimming,
And they do not come back
But stay deep at the bottom of the cold Baltic.
Tourists are usually so brave
But locals know better how to avoid the grave.

Have a walk near the coast after an evening tea.
Hear the waves — they sound like poetry.

Feed the loud gulls
And pigeons as well,
Fighting among themselves for food.
Then inhale the sea air
Which will not save you from longing
But you can at least try
To get rid of this feeling while the gulls cry.
Finding yourself in this coastal town
Then watching the sea run down.

The Unbearable Hardness of Being

We are so tired of being here.
To see everything,
To try everything
Then to forget everything.

And the fire went out
In this night hour.
We are waiting at dusk for fate
Under the oppression
Of other people's passions

In a strange crowd of people
Where you feel even more lonely
Than if you were actually alone.

Nevertheless,
All of this is still not enough.
To be completely gone
From this world
With its unbearable hardness of being

Without even the chance to be asked
If we would like it
From the beginning of our existence.

Autumn

Rain adagio,
Golden leaves, the same trees.

This autumn
As the year's most creative time
Gives hope of burning in a fire of tongues
Without the flaws that before tormented
And will bring the Muse
Which one can't buy in a store.

Heady foliage spirit
And the stuffy smell of pines.
The special look of autumn cottages
And the awe in the trees
And a cry in the sky.
Wandering without a goal through the forest,
As if I repent of something.
The shade of the leaves is poisonous
And now the poems flow from heaven
In a spontaneous pack.

The heavenly gaze has gone.
It brought the foliage for the fire
And bony rows of birches.
All the words were said,

All the songs sounded off
And late autumn stands like a verdict.
Such a proper time
To accept the fatality
Of the word ‘inevitability’.

Nocturnal Reflections

Uncharted jubilation
Of these lunar nights.
From ignorance to the joy of knowledge,
Desperately waiting to see a falling star.

And exposed to truth in the soul,
As if melting in a timid shade.
How does one revive oneself,
And feel alive again?

Warm, soulful touch of the night
Creating the magic of the moment.
Everything made in heaven should be right,

In the heart's sweet thaws,
Joy is beating and attraction is acute.
The star of life's milestones
Scrolls through the night
Decidedly cordially.

Try to understand the invalidity of a life
And escape from the bustle of the world
And flee to then watch
How your ordinariness
Fights with the desire to create magic.

We (24.02.2022)

“Not everything is black and white", they said.
“It can be also grey"
And, fully burdened,
What can we do besides cry and pray?

And now we are in the twilight of our destiny,
Stuck due to those with no regrets,
Those with no shame — just pure ambitions.

We hear their silly speeches;
Like in the worst nightmares but with new
villains and witches.
We might forgive them, but not forget.
Just be patient and wait,
Until they walk with us instead.

Who are they who are still living, but not
loving?
Who doesn't see others as themselves?

Captive is the whole new world
While they think what else could have been sold
And there is only one who foments war.

Meanwhile in the night sky,

The last, loneliest star has fallen.
Looking for a ray of a hope on thorns,
Watching colourful strange dreams,
Appearing to become real, it seems.
Crying, laughing, and not giving up.

We are the ones who just want a peaceful sky
Over our heads, with one prayer and love.
Dreaming of the sun as always above.
Even if we leave, we will surely come back.

www.ingramcontent.com/pod-product-compliance
Lightning Source LLC
Chambersburg PA
CBHW062204160726
48282CB00027B/996
* 9 7 8 9 3 5 7 6 1 0 3 5 3 *